COOL COOKIE & CAKE DECORATING *with* KIDS

TECHNIQUES AND PROJECTS FOR TEACHING KIDS, TEENS, AND TOTS

QUARRY

Inspiring | Educating | Creating | Entertaining

Brimming with creative inspiration, how-to projects, and useful information to enrich your everyday life, Quarto Knows is a favorite destination for those pursuing their interests and passions. Visit our site and dig deeper with our books into your area of interest: Quarto Creates, Quarto Cooks, Quarto Homes, Quarto Lives, Quarto Drives, Quarto Explores, Quarto Gifts, or Quarto Kids.

© 2015 Copyright
© 2014 Creative Publishing international, Inc.

First published in 2014 by
Creative Publishing international, Inc.,
an imprint of The Quarto Group
100 Cummings Center, Suite 265-D
Beverly, MA 01915, USA.
T (978) 282-9590 F (978) 283-2742
QuartoKnows.com

Creative Publishing international, Inc. titles are also
available at discount for retail, wholesale, promotional,
and bulk purchase. For details, contact the Special
Sales Manager by email at specialsales@quarto.com
or by mail at The Quarto Group, Attn: Special Sales
Manager, 100 Cummings Center, Suite 265-D,
Beverly, MA 01915, USA.

ISBN: 978-0-7603-7380-4

10 9 8 7 6 5 4 3 2 1

The information within this book was previously pub-
lished under the title *Decorate Cakes, Cupcakes, and
Cookies with Kids* by Autumn Carpenter (Creative
Publishing international, Inc., 2014).

Library of Congress Cataloging-in-Publication Data
Available under *Decorate Cakes, Cupcakes, and Cookies
with Kids* by Autumn Carpenter.

Copy Editor: Catherine Broberg

Proofreader: Karen Ruth

Book Design and Page Layout: tabula rasa graphic
design (www.trgraphicdesign.com)

Photographs: Dan Brand

Printed in Singapore

CONTENTS

chapter 1 • baking techniques

Baking a Cake and Cupcakes **4**

Baking Cupcakes **6**

Filling Cakes and Cupcakes **8**

chapter 2 • decorating techniques

Buttercream and Rolled Fondant Basics **10**

Food Color **12**

Icing Cakes and Cupcakes **13**

Covering Cakes and Cupcakes with Rolled Fondant **15**

Using Pastry Bags **17**

Piping Using Tips **18**

Rolling and Baking Cookies **22**

Icing Cookies **24**

Coordinating Party Treats **26**

chapter 3 • themed menus

Soccer Cake and Cookies **28**

Monster Bash, Monster Cupcakes **34**

Tropical Luau **38**

Festive Party Cake and Treats **42**

About the Author **48**

A WELL-BAKED CAKE that tastes great will make your beautifully decorated cake even better. Mixing a cake from scratch can be a bit time consuming but is rewarding. This book does not provide cake recipes. Find recipes by visit baking websites or ask a loved one to share a favorite cake recipe. Store-bought cake mixes are another alternative. Such mixes produce delicious, moist cakes and are convenient for beginning decorators. Simply follow the instructions on the cake mix box. The instructions on the boxes from major baking companies are clear, concise, and easy for children to follow.

Baking a Cake

Follow these general baking instructions for most cake pans. Dozens of shapes, sizes, and pan materials can be found in cake decorating supply stores. Novelty cake pans are available in several themes and popular licensed characters.

1. Preheat the oven according to the recipe's instructions. Using a pastry brush, generously spread pan grease thoroughly in the pan. Pan grease is available at cake and candy supply stores. If pan grease is unavailable, substitute solid vegetable shortening and then dust with all-purpose flour.

2. Prepare the cake batter according to the recipe's instructions. Pour the batter into the cake pan, filling the pan just over half full.

3. Place the filled pan in the preheated oven on the center rack. Bake according to the recipe's instructions. Check to see if the cake is done by inserting a cake tester into the center of the cake. If the cake tester comes out clean or with a few cake crumbs, the cake is done. If the tester comes out with batter, the cake is not thoroughly baked. Leave the cake in the oven and test after a minute or two. After the cake is baked, remove the pan from the oven and place on a cooling rack. Allow the cake to cool in the pan for 10 minutes. After cooling for 10 minutes, run a knife along the edge of the pan to loosen the sides.

4. When the pan is cool enough to handle, place a second cooling rack on top of the cake pan, sandwiching the pan between the cooling racks. Hold on to the two cooling racks tightly and flip over the pan.

More to Know

A single-layer cake is a cake baked and then decorated. These cakes are typically 1½" to 2" (3.8 to 5.1 cm) tall. A two-layer cake is a cake with two baked cakes placed on top of one another, usually with filling in between the layers. Two-layer cakes are generally 3" to 4" (7.6 to 10.2 cm) tall.

5. Place the cooling racks on the counter and remove the top cooling rack. Gently lift the cake pan. Allow the cake to cool completely before decorating, or the icing will melt.

6. If the cake is domed, use a cake slicer to cut off the top of dome.

Important

- *Thoroughly grease and flour the cake pan to prevent the cake from sticking to the pan when you are trying to release it. Extra grease and flour should be used on cake pans with embossed designs. Before releasing the cake from the pan, allow the pan to cool about 10 minutes. The pan should be warm, but not hot. If the cake is released too soon after baking, the cake may crack. If too much time passes before removing the cake, the cake may stick to the pan.*

- *If the cake has a sunken middle, the cake is likely underbaked. If the cake did not rise while baking, the batter may have been overmixed. Opening the oven door during baking may also cause the cake to deflate.*

Baking Cupcakes (see images above)

Hundreds of baking cups are available in many themes and colors. If a dark cake is used, the baking cup design may not be visible. It is best to use white cake batter if you want the design on the baking cup to show. A scoop is a useful tool when filling cupcake cavities. It keeps the filling process clean while scooping even amounts into each cavity. Use a 2-ounce scoop for standard cupcakes. Use a ⅓ cup scoop for jumbo cupcakes.

1. Line a cupcake pan with baking cups. Follow the recipe's instructions for preheating the oven and mixing the cake batter. Use a cookie scoop to fill the baking cups. The cups should be a little over half full.

2. Place the filled cupcake pan in the preheated oven and bake according to the recipe's instructions. Set the timer for 18 minutes or according to the recipe instructions. Check to see if the cupcakes are done by inserting a cake tester into the center of a cupcake. If the cake tester comes out clean or with a few cake crumbs, the cupcakes are done. If the tester comes out with batter, the cupcakes are not thoroughly baked. Leave the cupcakes in the oven and test within another minute or two or until the cake tester comes out clean. After the cupcakes are baked, remove the pan from the oven and place the pan on a cooling rack. Allow the pan to cool for 10 minutes. When the pan is cool enough to handle, remove the cupcakes and place them on a cooling rack. Allow the cupcakes to cool completely before decorating, or the icing will melt.

Adding Color to Cake Batter (see images on facing page)

Adding color to cake batter is an easy way to create a fun, vibrant surprise when the cake or cupcake is cut. Start with a white cake mix or white cake recipe. Use electric gel food colors for the brightest cakes.

1. Follow instructions for mixing the cake batter, using a white cake recipe or a white cake mix. Stir in food color. Pour the batter into the pan.

2. Make each layer a different color for an awesome presentation when the cake is cut.

3. If more than one color is desired, separate the batter into bowls for however many colors are desired. You can use several bowls and add color to each to make bright and colorful rainbow cupcakes. Add a scoop of each color until the baking cup is filled just over half full.

4. Enjoy your colorful creation!

Cupcakes (based on one cake mix)	Amount of Filling Needed	Icing Needed: Spread	Icing Needed: Piped	Bake Temp	Bake Time
96 mini cupcakes	1 cup (250 mL)	4 cups (1 L) 2 tsp. (10 mL) per cupcake	6 cups (1.5 L) 1 Tb. (15 mL) per cupcake	350°F (175°C)	8–10 min
24 standard cupcakes	1 cup (250 mL)	3 cups (750 mL) 2 Tb. (25 mL) per cupcake	4½ cups (1.125 L) 3 Tb. (50 mL) per cupcake	350°F (175°C)	18–24 min
7 jumbo cupcakes	¾ cup (175 mL)	1½ cups (375 mL) 3 Tb. (50 mL) per cupcake	2 cups (500 mL) 4 Tb. (59 mL) per cupcake	350°F (175°C)	20–25 min

Cupcake Chart

The chart above is based on cupcakes made from one standard cake mix which contains four to six cups (960 mL to 1.4 L) of batter and will bake approximately 96 mini cupcakes, 24 standard cupcakes, or 7 jumbo cupcakes. Cupcakes will take less icing if the icing is spread on the cupcake versus icing piped with a tip. If additional details will be piped with icing, double the amount of icing needed. All of the figures are approximate.

SURPRISE YOUR GUESTS by using a filling in the cake or cupcakes. The filling can be buttercream icing (or your favorite icing), pastry fillings (available at cake supply stores), or even ice-cream toppings such as hot fudge.

Filling a Cake

1. Fill a pastry bag with buttercream icing the same color that will be used on the outside of the cake. With tip #1A, pipe a dam of icing around the edge of the bottom layer of the cake. This dam will prevent the filling from oozing out the sides.

2. Squirt filling in the center of the cake. Spread the filling to the edges of the dam.

3. Aligning the layer, gently place the top layer on the bottom layer of cake.

More to Know

An apple corer is an ideal size to fill a standard size cupcake (left). Also shown is a cupcake plunger that works well for a jumbo size cupcake (right).

Filling Cupcakes

1. Allow the baked cupcakes to cool completely. When the cupcakes are cool, use a cupcake corer or an apple corer (shown) to remove the center of the cupcakes.

2. Press the trigger of the cupcake corer, or use the apple corer press to release the cut center.

3. Fill a pastry bag fitted with tip #2A with your favorite filling. Pipe the filling into the hollowed center of the cupcake, filling almost to the top.

BUTTERCREAM AND ROLLED FONDANT BASICS

BUTTERCREAM AND ROLLED FONDANT are used on the cake, cookie, and cupcake projects throughout this book. Buttercream is a fluffy, sweet icing that is either spread onto the cake or treat with a spatula or piped into fun textures or shapes using a pastry bag fitted with a cake decorating tip. Rolled fondant is a sweet, chewy icing that is rolled flat using a rolling pin and then formed over the cake or cut to fit a cookie or cupcake. Using rolled fondant is similar to working with clay. It can be cut into fun shapes, hand molded, or rolled in strips to form bows, loops, or stripes. When creating your own projects, use either icing or a combination of the two. For example, if the theme cake is covered in rolled fondant and has accents with rolled fondant, but you prefer the flavor of buttercream, simply ice the cake with buttercream and decorate it with rolled fondant accents.

Buttercream Icing

Buttercream is a traditional icing that is very sweet and fluffy. The icing will crust on the outside, but remain creamy on the inside. Buttercream is available premade at cake supply stores, or follow the recipe. The recipe includes hi-ratio shortening, which is available from specialty bakery supply stores and online sources. Baker's (hi-ratio) shortening is a shortening produced to replace butter. Use it instead of solid vegetable shortening to produce an icing with a fine, smooth, and creamy texture without a greasy aftertaste. Solid vegetable shortening may affect the icing consistency. For a bright white buttercream, choose clear butter and vanilla flavor. Pure vanilla will give the icing an ivory hue. Do not whip the icing on medium or high speed after the ingredients are blended. Doing so will add extra air into the icing, causing bubbles.

Buttercream Recipe

½ cup (120 mL) high-ratio shortening
4 cups (520 g) powdered sugar, sifted
5 tablespoons (75 mL) water
½ teaspoon (2.5 mL) salt
1 teaspoon (5 mL) vanilla flavoring
½ teaspoon (2.5 mL) almond flavoring
¼ teaspoon 1.5 mL) butter flavoring

In a large bowl, combine the ingredients; beat on low speed until well blended. Continue beating on low speed for 10 minutes or until very creamy. Keep the bowl covered to prevent the icing from drying out. Unused icing can be kept in the refrigerator up to 6 weeks. Rewhip stored icing on low speed before using.

Chocolate Buttercream Recipe

Make a delicious chocolate buttercream icing simply by adding cocoa powder to the buttercream recipe. Add 1 cup (110 g) of cocoa powder to the buttercream recipe above. The cocoa powder may cause the buttercream to stiffen. Add a small amount of water to achieve the desired consistency.

Storing Buttercream

Cakes that are iced and decorated with buttercream will most likely form a crust. Humidity may affect the icing's ability to crust. An iced and decorated cake with buttercream can be kept at room temperature for three or four days. Extreme warm temperatures can cause the icing to soften and melt. Refrigerating iced and decorated cakes with buttercream may cause condensation, making colors bleed.

Rolled Fondant

Rolled fondant is used to cover cakes and to create accents. The icing has a chewy texture. Before covering a cake with fondant, the cake should have an undericing. Icing the cake first in buttercream gives the cake a smooth base while adding sweetness and sealing in moisture. Recipes are available for making rolled fondant, but it can be difficult to achieve the proper texture. Before attempting a recipe, try using commercial rolled fondant to become familiar with the texture and consistency. The flavor of commercial rolled fondant will vary tremendously. Gum paste is used to make accents that hold up better than rolled fondant. Gum paste sets very hard and should not be eaten. Purchase commercial gum paste, or make an easy gum paste by kneading 1 tablespoon of food-grade tylose into rolled fondant. Wrap the tylose gum paste tightly and allow the paste to rest for several hours. Use candy clay as an alternative to rolled fondant for accents on cakes but not as a cake covering. All forms of edible clay including rolled fondant, gum paste, and candy clay will dry out quickly. Keep the edible pastes tightly wrapped and sealed when not working with them.

Rolled Fondant Recipe

½ (120 g) cup cream

2 tablespoons 30 mL) unflavored gelatin

¾ (175 mL) cup glucose

2 tablespoons (28 g) butter

2 tablespoons (25 mL) glycerin

2 teaspoons (10 mL) clear vanilla flavor

2 teaspoons (10 mL) clear butter flavor

1 teaspoon (5 mL) clear almond flavor

approximately 9 cups (1 kg) powdered sugar

Pour the cream into a small saucepan. Sprinkle gelatin on the cream and cook on low until the gelatin has dissolved. Add the glucose, butter, glycerin, and flavorings. Heat until the butter is melted. Set aside. Sift the powdered sugar. Place 7 cups (770g)

of the powdered sugar in a mixing bowl. Pour the cream mixture over the powdered sugar and mix slowly with a dough hook until the powdered sugar is thoroughly mixed. Add the additional 2 cups (220 g) of powdered sugar. The fondant will be very sticky, but should hold its shape. Lay a sheet of plastic wrap on the counter, and coat with a thin layer of vegetable shortening. Wrap the fondant in the greased plastic wrap and allow to set for 24 hours. After 24 hours, the fondant should be less sticky. If not, add more powdered sugar.

Rolling Rolled Fondant for Cutting Accents

Dust the work surface with powdered sugar. Knead and soften the rolled fondant. Roll the fondant, lifting and turning it after every other roll. If the fondant is sticking to the surface, add more powdered sugar. Do not flip the rolled fondant over. Use perfection strips to keep the rolled fondant an even thickness. The rolled fondant should be rolled using the thinnest strips (2 mm thick) for accents on cakes. Daintier accents should be rolled thinner than 2 mm. A pasta machine is ideal for rolling fondant very thin to make dainty accents. Use medium strips (4 mm) when covering cookies with rolled fondant.

FOOD COLOR

ROLLED FONDANT AND BUTTERCREAM icing are available pre-colored at cake supply stores for convenience. Purchasing icing pre-colored keeps your hands and clothing free of food color stains. However, it may be more cost effective to purchase white icing and add color using food colors. Concentrated colors such as gel colors and powder colors are best suited for coloring icings and fondant. If using liquid food color, excessive color may be needed, which may affect the consistency of the buttercream and rolled fondant. Even when using gels or powdered colors, it can be difficult to obtain dark colors such as red, brown, and black. The shade of each tube or jar of food color will vary from pale to deep depending on the amount of color added to the icing. Too much color and the icing may taste bitter and may also leave a tinge on mouths when eaten. When mixing black or brown, begin by adding cocoa powder to the icing to achieve a brown base; this will eliminate the need to add excessive amounts of black or brown food color. When mixing red, start with a no-taste red and add a vibrant red, such as super red. If mixing powdered colors into the buttercream or rolled fondant, blend a small amount of vegetable shortening with the powdered food color. When coloring chocolate candy coating, use an oil-based food color. Water-based coloring will cause the chocolate to thicken.

Food color will stain clothes, countertops, and hands. Wear aprons when adding food color to avoid staining clothing. Water and soap will remove coloring from hands, although it may take several washings. Use bleach or powdered cleanser on countertops to remove stains. Test an unseen area of the counter top first.

Colors may fade if the decorated cake is exposed to light. Natural sunlight and fluorescent lights will produce the harshest effects, but even common household lighting may cause the colors on the cake to fade. Keep the cake in a cool, dark room to avoid fading. Storing the cake in a covered box will also reduce the fading.

When moisture affects the icing, colors may bleed. Keep iced cakes in a loosely wrapped box until ready to serve. An airtight container will cause condensation to form, which may cause bleeding. Placing a cake in the refrigerator may also cause the colors to bleed. When piping on icing, allow contrasting colors to form a crust before adding an adjoining color.

Adding Color to Buttercream Icing (see image below)

Dark colors in buttercream icing may intensify upon setting. Allow the icing to set for 2 or 3 hours to see true color.

1. Add a small amount of food color to the icing. Use a toothpick to remove color in jars, or if the color is in tubes, squeeze the color into the icing.

2. Blend until all color is thoroughly incorporated. There should be no streaks of color. If the color is too dark, add white icing. If the color is too light, add a little more color.

Adding Color to Rolled Fondant

Excessive color may cause the rolled fondant to become sticky. Knead in additional powdered sugar if the food color changes the consistency. Avoid using liquid food color, as it requires a significant amount of coloring to obtain bright colors. Concentrated gel or powdered coloring works best.

1. Knead and soften the rolled fondant. With concentrated food color, add a dot of color.

2. Knead until there are no streaks of color remaining.

ICING CAKES AND CUPCAKES

Icing a Cake

It takes practice and patience to ice a cake with a smooth, clean finish. Place the cake on a turntable to help you manipulate the spatula with consistent pressure. First apply a crumb coat, which seals the crumbs and prevents them from mixing with the buttercream. When crumb coating, use two bowls; one for icing that is free of crumbs, and the other to scrape the spatula as you remove excess icing and crumbs.

1. Place the cake on a cardboard the same size as the cake. Mix icing for the crumb coat by thinning buttercream with a small amount of water (about 1 teaspoon of water to 1 cup of buttercream). It should be just thin enough to barely see crumbs underneath. Spread the thinned icing on the cake, also covering the cardboard. Allow the crumb coat to form a crust (20–45 minutes). Dispose of left-over thinned icing.

2. After the crumb coat has set, place a generous amount of buttercream icing on the top of the cake.

3. With a long spatula, spread the icing on the top using long strokes and gliding toward the edge.

4. Apply icing to the side of the cake, holding the spatula perpendicular to the turntable. Blend the icing on the top with the icing on the sides.

5. Glide the spatula along the top and sides of the cake to smooth.

6. After the icing forms a crust (approximately 45 minutes), gently roll over any areas that are not smooth with a pastry roller.

DECORATING TECHNIQUES

13

Icing Cupcakes

Icing can be spread or piped onto cupcakes. When piping cupcakes, use an icing that holds its shape, such as buttercream, or the details will be lost. Refer to the icing chart on page 7 to determine how much icing is needed.

Piping Icing onto Cupcakes (see images below)

1. Allow the cupcake to cool completely. Fit a pastry bag with a tip that has a large opening. Tips #1A, #1M, or #8B work well for piping icing onto cupcakes. Fill the pastry bag with buttercream icing. Pipe a ring around the outside edge of the cupcake. Continue piping, creating a swirl on top of the cupcake.

2. Each tip gives a unique piped design as shown, left to right: #1M, #1A, #8B.

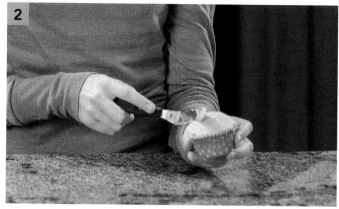

Spreading Icing onto Cupcakes (see images above)

1. Scoop a generous amount of icing onto the top of a baked and cooled cupcake.

2. Evenly spread the icing to the edges of the cupcake.

COVERING CAKES AND CUPCAKES WITH ROLLED FONDANT

Covering a Cake with Rolled Fondant

Covering a cake with rolled fondant provides a smooth, clean appearance. Try to complete all the steps within 5–7 minutes. The fondant may develop tiny cracks or "elephant skin" if too much time elapses. An undericing provides extra sweetness and a clean, smooth surface. The instructions are for a cake with buttercream underneath, but other icings may be used. To allow the cake to be easily moved after it is covered, place it on a cardboard the same size as the cake. Powdered sugar or cornstarch can be used on the countertop to keep the fondant from sticking. When working with children, use powdered sugar, as it will blend into the fondant; cornstarch does not blend and will cause white powdery spots on the fondant. Too much cornstarch can also quickly dry out the fondant. When rolling fondant, be sure to rotate it often so fondant holds an even shape. Avoid flipping the fondant, as residue from the countertop will stick to the fondant.

1. Bake and cool the cake. Place the cake on a cardboard the same size. With thinned buttercream, crumb coat the cake; then ice the cake following instructions on page 13. After the buttercream has crusted, brush the top with piping gel. Dust the work surface with powdered sugar. Knead and soften the rolled fondant. Roll the fondant, lifting and turning the fondant every other roll. If the fondant is sticking to the surface, add additional powdered sugar. Do not flip the rolled fondant over. Continue rolling until the fondant is approximately ⅛" (3 mm) thick. Roll out a circle of fondant so it is the diameter of the cake plus the height of the cake doubled plus 1" (2.5 cm); this will provide enough fondant to cover the cake even if the fondant is not perfectly centered. For example, the cake shown is 8" (20.3 cm) in diameter and 4" (10.2 cm) tall. The amount of rolled fondant needed is 8 + 4 + 4 + 1 = 17" (20.3 + 10.2 + 10.2 + 2.5 cm = 43.2 cm).

2. Lift the rolled fondant using the rolling pin. Starting at the base of the cake, unroll the fondant onto the cake.

3. Lift and shift the sides to eliminate any creases. Take care not to stretch and pull the fondant.

4. Secure the edges by pressing palms against the sides of the cake.

5. With a mini pizza cutter, remove any excess fondant.

6. With your nondominant hand, rest one fondant smoother on the top of the cake to hold the cake steady and to smooth the top of the cake. Do not apply pressure or the smoother will impress lines. Smooth the sides with another fondant smoother. Spread buttercream on a cake plate or cake cardboard. Lift the cake using a jumbo spatula and place on the cake plate.

Covering Cupcakes with Rolled Fondant

Add a smooth finish to cupcakes with rolled fondant. Rolled fondant is a bit heavy for a handheld treat, so be sure to roll the fondant thin when covering cupcakes. A thin layer of buttercream icing underneath the fondant adds additional sweetness. A 3" (7.6 cm) round cookie cutter will cover cupcakes with a slight dome. Cupcakes that are slightly underfilled or overfilled will require a smaller or larger disk of fondant. It is helpful to have a set of round cookie cutters with a range of sizes.

1. Bake and cool the cupcakes. Fit a pastry bag with tip #2A. Fill the bag with buttercream or any icing that can be piped. Pipe a swirl on the cupcake, leaving approximately ½" (1.3 cm) all around the edge. Dust the work surface with powdered sugar. Knead and soften the rolled fondant. Roll the fondant, lifting and turning the fondant every other roll. If the fondant is sticking to the surface, add additional powdered sugar. Do not flip the rolled fondant over. Continue rolling until the fondant is approximately ⅛" (3 mm) thick. Use a cookie cutter to cut circles. Place the cut circles on top of the just-iced cupcakes. Smooth the top and sides of the covered cupcake with your palm.

Important

CIRCUMFERENCE AND DIAMETER

It is often necessary to determine the circumference or diameter of round cakes. For accuracy, measure after icing a cake or covering a cake with rolled fondant. For example, after an 8" (20 cm) cake is covered with fondant, it may have a diameter of 8¼" (21 cm).

Diameter: *The diameter is the line that passes through the center of a circle. Most round cake pans are measured by their diameter. An 8" (20 cm) cake pan will be 8" (20 cm) in diameter.*

Circumference: *The circumference is the measurement around the cake. This figure is important to know when wrapping fondant ribbon strips or adding a decorative ribbon around the cake board. The circumference is figured by taking the diameter of the pan (or board) and multiplying it by 3.14 (or π).*
An 8" (20 cm) cake has a circumference of 25.1" (64 cm). If wrapping a cake with a fondant ribbon, 25.1" (64 cm) will be required.

Circumference

Diameter

USING PASTRY BAGS

CLEAR, DISPOSABLE PASTRY BAGS are ideal for children to use, as they can see all the colors to choose from and there is little cleanup when finished. Reusable pastry bags are also available. The tips of the bags can be cut and a cake decorating tip dropped in. One-third of the tip should be showing. If more than one-third is showing, the bag may tear. A coupler can be used to change tips without filling a new bag. If only one tip is needed for a single color, it is not necessary to use a coupler; however, a coupler does keep icing from seeping. When children are using pastry bags, be sure to secure the pastry bag with a rubber band or icing bag tie to prevent the icing from bursting from the top of the bag.

Using a Coupler

1. Cut the reusable pastry bag or disposable pastry bag so that 1 or 2 threads are showing on the coupler base when the coupler base is dropped into the bag.

2. Drop the coupler into the bag. Pull the coupler tightly to secure. Place the tip on the coupler base. Twist the coupler screw top to tighten the tip in place.

Filling Pastry Bags

3. Drop the tip into the pastry bag or fit the pastry bag with a coupler and tip following instructions above. Fold the pastry bag over hands to form a cuff. The cuff fold should be 2" to 3" (5.1 to 7.6 cm). Scoop icing into the bag until it reaches the top of the cuff. Fill the bag about half full with icing. The more full the bag, the more difficult the bag is to control.

4. Squeeze the bag between your thumb and fingers and push the icing toward the bottom of the bag. Twist the bag where the icing begins. To control the icing, grip the bag with your dominant hand. Use the tip of your index finger on your nondominant hand to guide the bag. Squeeze the icing while guiding the bag.

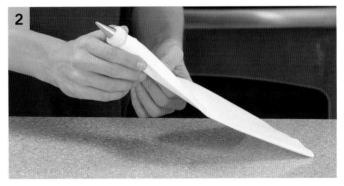

PIPING USING TIPS

ADD TEXTURE to cookies, cakes, and cupcakes by piping designs with icing. An icing that holds its shape, such a buttercream, is a must. Successful piping depends on using the right amount of consistent pressure. Practice on a sheet of parchment paper using various amounts of pressure. It is important to keep the tip clean and free of icing buildup for crisp and precise piping. If piping a border on a cake, place the cake on a turntable and rotate to achieve an even, consistent border.

Dots

Use piped dots for polka dots, flower petals, flower centers, or a dot border. The most popular tips for piping dots are #2, #3, #4, #6, #8, and #10. However, it is handy to have nearly every round-opening tip. The smaller the number, the smaller the piped dot.

1. Start with the pastry bag at a 90° angle just above the surface. Squeeze the pastry bag to pipe a dot, holding the tip steady as the icing forms around the tip. Continue squeezing the pastry bag until the dot is the desired size. Stop pressure and lift the pastry bag.

2. If there are small peaks after the dots are formed, gently press the peak with the tip of your index finger just before the icing forms a crust.

Stars and Flowers

Use piped stars for simple piped accents and easy borders. Stars are also commonly used on shaped theme cakes. Pipe stars close together to completely cover the cake. The most popular tips for piping stars are #16, #18, #21, and #32. The smaller the number, the smaller the piped star.

3. Start with the pastry bag at a 90° angle just above the surface. Squeeze the pastry bag to pipe a star, holding the tip steady as the icing forms around the tip. Continue squeezing

the pastry bag until the star is the desired size. The bag should not be lifted until the star is formed. Stop pressure and lift the pastry bag.

4. Make a flower by adding a small dot in a contrasting color to the center.

Leaves

Tips #350, #352, and #366 (large leaf) are used to pipe leaves. These tips look like a bird beak. When piping, remember to have 1 point of the "bird beak" on the work surface. Do not pipe with the "bird beak" on its side.

5. Position the pastry bag at a 45° angle. One point of the tip should be touching the surface. Squeeze the pastry bag with a short burst of pressure to attach the leaf. Gradually release pressure and lift the tip. Stop pressure and lift the pastry bag.

Grass

Tip #233 is used to pipe grass or fur. When piping grass, be sure the tip is kept clean, or the strands will come out in a blob. Most metal grass tips have ridges around the fine holes. The ridges make it difficult to keep the end of the metal tip clean. The plastic grass tip is smooth without ridges, which makes it easier to keep clean. The length and style of grass can vary. To pipe long strands of grass, attach grass with a burst of pressure. Continue with a lot of pressure while lifting.

6. Position the pastry bag at a 90° angle. The tip should be touching the surface. Squeeze the pastry bag with a short burst of pressure to attach the grass. Continue with pressure and drag the tip upward. Stop pressure and lift the pastry bag. Pipe the grass close together so there are no gaps.

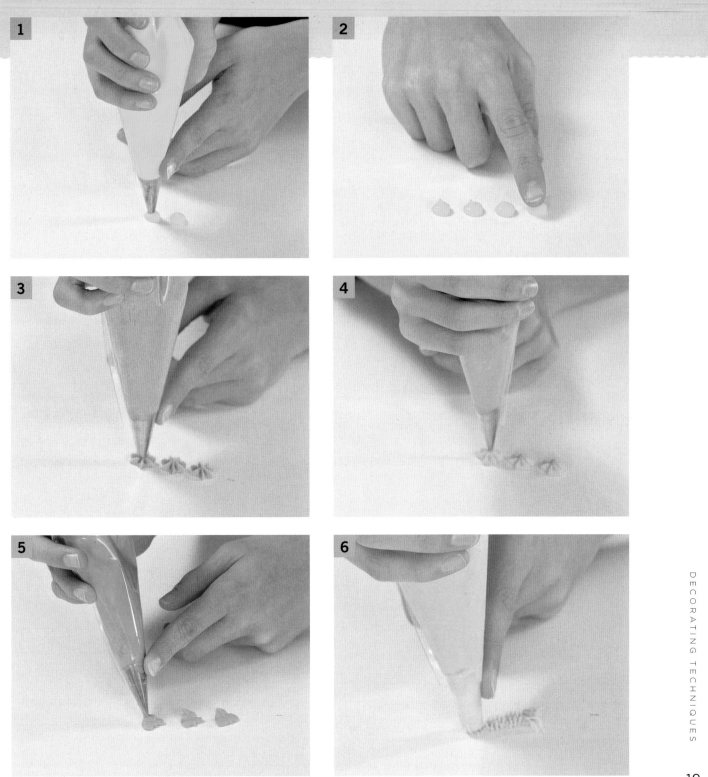

Continue piping with uninterrupted pressure, piping a line or curve for the letter or number. Let the icing flow from the bag naturally just above the surface. Do not drag the tip on the cake. Stop pressure and touch the surface to attach the end of the letter or number.

Shell Border

A shell border is the most common border used on cakes. Tip #21 produces a border with deep groves, while tip #32 creates a border with finer grooves. Use tip #18 for smaller, daintier borders.

8. Position the pastry bag at a 45° angle, nearly touching the surface. Apply pressure while moving the tip forward slightly. Move back to the starting point, gradually release pressure, and drag the tip to form a shell. Stop pressure and pull the tip away. Start the next shell at the tail of the first shell.

Teardrop Border

Use a tip with a round opening, such as tip #10, to form a teardrop-shaped border. Tip #12 will produce a larger designed border, while tip #8 (shown) will create a daintier border.

9. Position the pastry bag at a 45° angle, nearly touching the surface. Squeeze the pastry bag to form a ball. Gradually release pressure and drag the tip to form a teardrop. Start the next teardrop at the end of the first teardrop.

Zigzag Border

Use a star tip to pipe this fun border. You can vary the design simply by piping the points closer together or by stretching the distance between the points. Use tip #18 for a nice size zigzag border.

10. Position the pastry bag at a 45° angle, nearly touching the surface. With steady pressure move the tip in a zigzag pattern. When the border is complete, stop applying pressure and lift the pastry bag.

Writing

Use a tip with a round opening, such as tip #2, #3, or #4, for writing on the cake. The smaller the tip number, the daintier the writing. If the lines are breaking when piping, you are not applying enough pressure or are moving the piping bag too fast. If too much pressure is applied, the lines may have wiggles or loops.

7. Position the pastry bag at a 45° angle. Squeeze the pastry bag to release the icing, touch the surface, and then lift the icing just above the surface while continuing with pressure.

CUTOUT COOKIES are not just for the holidays. Decorate shaped cookies to coordinate with the party cake. Cookie cutters are available in hundreds of shapes. Plastic cutters are great to use for younger children because there are no sharp edges. Metal cutters are most commonly available in tin, stainless steel, and copper. Copper cutters tend to be formed thicker, making them less sharp than other metals.

Cookie Recipes

The two recipes included in this chapter have a subtle sweetness that is enhanced with icing. Both cookies have a tender crumb; not too soft and not too crisp. The Buttery Sugar Cookie recipe must be chilled at least 2 hours before rolling to firm the cream cheese and butter. The Chocolate Cutout Cookie recipe can be used immediately after mixing. The chocolate cookie tends to crumble a bit when rolling, and the cookies can easily be overbaked because the edges do not brown. Baked cookies, with or without icing, are best eaten within 7 to 10 days.

Buttery Sugar Cookie

1 cup (2 sticks [225 g]) unsalted butter, softened

3 ounces (85 g) cream cheese, softened

¾ cup (170 g) sugar

1 egg

1 teaspoon (5 mL) vanilla

3 cups (330 g) all-purpose flour

Combine the butter and cream cheese with an electric mixer on medium speed for 2 or 3 minutes or until well blended. Scrape the sides of the bowl.

Add the sugar. Continue to blend on medium speed until the mixture is light and fluffy. Add the vanilla and mix.

Add the egg, mixing on low until thoroughly blended. Scrape the bowl.

Add the flour, 1 cup (110 g) at a time. Scrape the bowl after adding each cup. Mix until just incorporated. Do not overmix, or the dough will toughen.

Divide the dough into two equal portions. Flatten the dough into two patties that are approximately 1½" (3.8 cm) thick. Wrap the patties with plastic wrap and refrigerate at least 2 hours or until firm.

Preheat the oven to 375°F (190°C). Roll out the dough and cut the cookies (page 23). Bake the cookies for 9 to 11 minutes or until the edges are very lightly browned.

Yields 36 (3" to 4" [7.6 to 10.2 cm] cookies)

Chocolate Cutout Cookies

1 cup (2 sticks [225 g]) butter, softened

1½ cup (340 g) sugar

2 eggs

2 teaspoons (10 mL) vanilla

3 cups (330 g) all-purpose flour

⅔ cup (75 g) unsweetened cocoa powder

½ teaspoon (2.5 mL) salt

Preheat the oven to 350°F (175°C). In a large bowl, stir together the flour, cocoa powder, and salt.

In a separate large bowl, combine the butter and sugar with an electric mixer on medium speed for 2 or 3 minutes or until the mixture is light and fluffy. Scrape down the sides of the bowl.

Add the eggs and vanilla and mix on low until thoroughly blended. Scrape the bowl.

Add the flour mixture, 1 cup (110 g) at a time. Scrape the bowl after adding each cup of flour. Mix until just incorporated. Do not overmix, or the dough will toughen.

Divide the dough into two equal portions. Flatten the dough into two patties that are approximately 1½" (3.8 cm) thick. Use the dough immediately, or refrigerate until ready to mold or roll.

Bake the cookies for 8 to 10 minutes or until no indentation is made when touched.

Yields 36 (3" to 4" [7.6 to 10.2 cm] cookies)

Rolling Cookie Dough and Cutting Shapes

A baked cookie provides a smooth surface for icing. Use perfection strips or a rolling pin with rings to achieve a cookie with an even surface. The icing used determines how thick the baked cookie should be. If the baked cookie is thin and the buttercream on the cookie is piled high, the buttercream will overpower the cookie. If covering the cookie in rolled fondant, the baked cookie should be at least twice as thick as the rolled fondant piece. For best results, the dough should be cool, but not too cold that it is difficult to roll. Take the dough out of the refrigerator an hour before rolling it.

1. Chill dough, if required in recipe. Place the cookie dough between perfection strips on the countertop dusted with flour. Roll over the strips, leveling the cookie dough. The dough may also be rolled on a silicone mat or a sheet of parchment paper. If the dough is sticking to the parchment paper, silicone mat, or countertop, lightly dust with as little flour as possible to avoid toughening the dough. If the dough is still sticking, try chilling the dough for 1 or 2 hours. If it is still sticking, you can add more flour to the dough, but it may toughen the baked cookie.

2. Press the cutter into the dough, cutting the shapes as close together as possible.

3. Remove the excess dough and transfer the cut shape to a cookie sheet lined with a silicone mat or parchment paper.

4. Bake the cookies according to the recipe instructions. After the cookies are baked, allow the cut shapes to cool approximately 3 to 4 minutes. Use a cookie spatula to gently transfer the warm, cut shapes to a cooling rack. Baked cookies will be fragile and soft to touch while they are still hot. Take extra care when transferring the baked cookie from the cookie sheet to the cooling rack. Allow the cookies to cool completely before decorating.

5. To insert a stick into cookies to make a cookie bouquet, follow steps 1–3 above. Insert the stick into the dough. Rest the stick on the cookie sheet at the base of the cookie dough. Hold the other end of the stick between the index finger and thumb of your dominant hand, and begin twisting and pushing the stick up into the cut cookie dough. Keep the stick as parallel to the cookie sheet as possible. Use the index finger of your nondominant hand to keep the stick from protruding through the cookie dough. Push until the stick is about three-fourths into the cut shape. Continue with step 4 above. If the cookie becomes loose from the stick after baking, add a bit of icing or melted chocolate coating to the back of the cookie, securing the stick.

ICING COOKIES

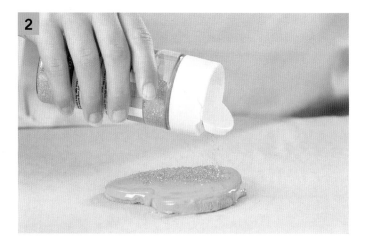

THREE ICINGS are covered in this section: chocolate coating, buttercream icing, and rolled fondant. A cookie coated in chocolate coating gives a delicious, smooth covering. Because the chocolate coating sets firm, these cookies are great for stacking. If the cookies are served outside and it is warm, the chocolate coating may melt. Buttercream icing on a cookie provides a sweetness like no other. Buttercream can also be piped onto cookies using the piping techniques on pages 18–21. Rolled fondant gives a covering with a clean, professional finish.

Dipping a Cookie in Chocolate Coating

1. Melt candy coating following directions on page 26. Hold on to the cookie and dip the top into the melted candy coating. After lifting the cookie out of the coating, turn your wrist so the coated cookie is facing you. Tap your wrist against the counter to smooth the chocolate coating.

2. Place the cookie on parchment paper to set. If sprinkles are desired, add them before the chocolate coating sets.

3. Smaller cookies may be immersed in the chocolate coating and then removed using a dipping tool.

4

Covering a Cookie with Rolled Fondant

4. Bake and cool cookies. Brush the top of the cookie with a very thin layer of piping gel. Knead and soften the rolled fondant. Dust the work surface with powdered sugar. Roll the fondant in between perfection strips, lifting and turning the fondant after every other roll. If the fondant is sticking to the surface, add more powdered sugar. Do not flip the rolled fondant over. Continue rolling until the fondant is approximately 2 to 4 mm thick. The baked cookie should be twice as thick as the rolled fondant or the rolled fondant will overpower the cookie. Cut the fondant with the same cutter used for the cookie.

Icing a Cookie with Buttercream

5. Scoop a generous amount of buttercream onto the cookie. Spread the icing across the cookie using a spatula at least the length and width of the cookie. Clean the spatula.

6. Hold the spatula perpendicular to the cookie and scrape along the side to clean the edge of the cookie.

5

6

COORDINATING PARTY TREATS

IMPRESS YOUR GUESTS by making delicious treats to coordinate with the cake or to give as party favors. Many of these treats are made with candy coating which is easy to use. Simply melt in the microwave and dip your treat into the melted candy. Chocolates and coatings have a very low melting point, so watch it carefully as it melts to prevent scorching. Using a bowl with a squared edge allows the chocolate coating to be easily poured into squeeze bottles. Small tubes filled with candy coating are called candy writers—use them to paint suckers or add details to cookies. This chapter covers coating pretzels and sandwich cookies, but almost any snack can be dipped in chocolate. Try graham crackers, popcorn, nuts, or even potato chips!

Melting Candy Coating

1. Place the candy wafers in a microwave-safe bowl. Put the bowl in the microwave. Turn on the microwave for 30 seconds. Remove the bowl from the microwave and stir. Put the bowl of wafers back into the microwave and turn on for 20 more seconds. Remove the bowl from the microwave and stir again.

2. Continue in this way by heating for 20 seconds, removing the bowl, and then stirring until all but a few wafers have melted. Stir until the unmelted wafers melt.

More to Know

- Keep the bowls of melted chocolate, filled squeeze bottles, parchment cones, and candy writers warm by placing them in an electric skillet on the lowest setting lined with several dry towels. The skillet should be warm to touch but not hot enough to burn or the chocolate will cook and burn instead of melt. Bottles and candy writers can also be placed in a heating pad set to low to keep the chocolate warm.

- A wide variety of colored candy coating can be purchased ready to use. If a color is desired that is not available, simply color the candy with an oil-based food color. Avoid using food color gels, pastes, and liquids, or the chocolate may thicken when color is added. You can use powdered food colors, but be sure to dissolve the powder in liquid vegetable shortening before adding to the chocolate.

General Molding (see images below)

1. Use candy writers to paint details inside of candy molds. Allow the candy to set at room temperature before adding adjoining colors. Only use candy writers to paint details. Do not use them for filling the entire cavity. The chocolate candy inside candy writers must be heated before using the tube. Place the candy writer tube in a heating pad for 1 hour before using. Keep the candy writers in the heating pad to prevent the candy from setting up in between use. If the tip of the candy writer clogs, use a straight pin to unclog.

2. Allow the details to set up at room temperature. Pour melted candy coating into a squeeze bottle. After the details have set, fill the rest of the mold using the candy from the squeeze bottle. Place the filled molds in the freezer to set. The time needed for the candy to set is determined by the thickness of the mold cavity. Thin candy pieces set up after a few minutes in the freezer, while thick pieces will take much longer. The candy should release from the mold with little effort.

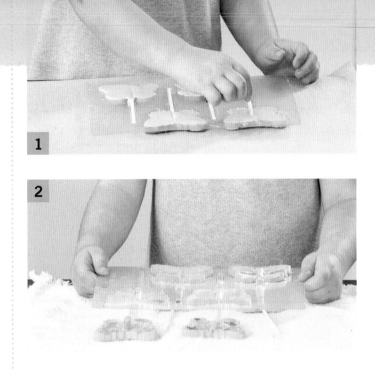

Chocolate Suckers (see images above)

1. Follow steps 1 and 2 for General Molding at left. Insert a sucker stick at least three-fourths into the filled cavity. Place the filled mold in the freezer for a few minutes.

2. When the suckers are ready, the candy will feel cold and the mold will be cloudy. Place a towel on the countertop. Turn over the sucker mold onto the towel to release the suckers. If the candy sticks to the mold when the mold is turned over, the candy is not ready. Return the mold to the freezer. If the candy cracks or breaks when the mold is turned over, the candy was left in the freezer too long.

SOCCER CAKE AND COOKIES

SOCCER BALL CAKE

You Will Need

soccer ball cake pan

9" (22.9 cm) cardboard

10" (25.4 cm) round cake pan

12" (30.5 cm) cake drum or cake plate

rolled fondant, blue, pink, and orange

flower plunger cutter

flower former

disposable pastry bags

6 cups (1.5 L) buttercream icing, electric green

¼ cup (60 mL) buttercream icing, gray

1 cup (250 mL) buttercream icing, black

3 cups (750 mL) buttercream icing, white

tip #233

tip #18

tip #4

piping gel

Techniques

Baking Cakes, page 4

Icing Cakes, page 13

Buttercream and Rolled Fondant Basics, page 10

Piping Using Tips, page 18

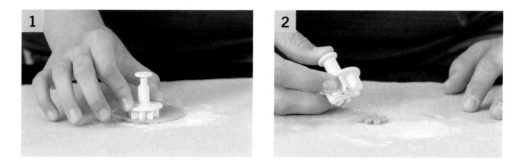

1. At least one day ahead of time, make the flowers for the cake. Dust the work surface with powdered sugar. Roll kneaded and softened rolled fondant thin. Using a flower plunger cutter, firmly press into the rolled fondant, holding the base of the cutter—do not hold onto the plunger when cutting.

2. Lift the cutter and gently run your finger along the edge of the cutter to ensure the cut is clean. Push the trigger to release the cut flower. If the cut flower remains on the work surface, use a spatula with a thin blade to lift it. Dust the surface with additional powdered sugar before cutting more flowers.

Important

The flowers around the buttercream grass border and on the soccer cookies should be made ahead of time. Or buy premade edible flowers, available at most cake decorating supply stores.

More To Know

Shaped cake pans, such as the soccer pan used here, are available in a variety of themes as well as popular television and movie characters. To decorate these cakes, use buttercream icing to outline shapes and then pipe stars to fill them in.

Younger Kids

Give a spatula to younger kids to stir all the different colors of buttercream. Be sure the kids are wearing an apron, as the colors may stain their clothes. The rolled fondant edible flowers can be made by kids of all ages. Kids can also place the flowers on the cookies and cake.

3. Place the cut flower in a flower former tray to shape the petals. Add a dot of piping gel in the center of the flower and place a candy bead or Sixlet in the center of the flower.

4. Bake a two-layer 10" (25.4 cm) round cake, following instructions on pages 4–5. Ice the cake with electric green buttercream, following instructions on page 13. Place the cake on a 12" (30.5 cm) board. Bake a cake using a soccer ball cake pan. Allow the cake to cool completely. Place the soccer ball cake on a 9" (22.9 cm) cardboard circle or a cardboard the same size or slightly smaller than the soccer ball. Gently place the cake onto the iced 10" (25.4 cm) cake.

5. Fit a pastry bag with tip #4. Fill the bag with gray icing. Outline the cake. To outline, touch the cake and gently squeeze the pastry bag to attach the icing. Continue squeezing, gently lift the bag, and pipe a line following the indentations shown on the baked cake. Stop pressure and touch the cake to attach the icing. Outline the entire cake.

6. Fit two pastry bags with tip #18. Fill one bag with black icing and the other with white icing. Fill in the outlined soccer ball with stars piped close together. To pipe a star,

hold the pastry bag just above the cake. Squeeze the bag to pipe a star. Continue squeezing the bag until the star is the desired size. Stop pressure and lift the bag. Pipe the stars side by side and very close together so there aren't any gaps that will show the cake underneath. Pipe the next row of stars between previously piped stars to eliminate gaps.

7. Fit a pastry bag with tip #233. Fill the bag with electric green icing. Pipe grass around the base of the soccer ball and around the bottom of the 10" (25.4 cm) cake. To pipe grass, hold the pastry bag at a 90° angle. The tip should be touching the iced cake. Squeeze the pastry bag with a short burst of pressure to attach the grass. Continue applying pressure and drag the tip upward. Stop pressure and lift the pastry bag. Pipe the grass close together to eliminate gaps.

8. Press rolled fondant flowers or premade flowers into the cake.

SOCCER BALL COOKIES

You Will Need

soccer cookie cutter texture set

rolled fondant in white and in colors desired for flowers (or use other edible flowers)

piping gel

food color marker, black

Techniques

Rolling and Baking Cookies, page 22

Rolled Fondant Basics, page 10

Icing Cookies, page 24

1. At least one day ahead of time, make the flowers for the cookies following steps 1–3 on pages 29–31. Bake and cool round cookies on a stick using the cutter from the soccer ball cookie cutter texture set. Roll the white fondant thin. Place the smooth, rolled side of the fondant on top of the soccer ball texture mat. With a lot of pressure, roll over the fondant.

2. Turn over the fondant and peel back the mat.

3. Use the same cutter that was used for baking the cookies to cut the soccer ball design.

4. Brush the cookie with a thin layer of piping gel. Place the cut fondant soccer ball on top of the cookie.

5. Allow several hours for the fondant to harden. When the fondant is firm, color in the textured details using a black food color marker.

6. Use piping gel to attach the edible flowers to the cookies.

More To Know

Some cookie cutters, such as the soccer ball, come with plastic mats with recessed lines that line up with the cutter. Use the mats to add texture and instant details to rolled fondant.

MONSTER BASH

★★

MONSTER CUPCAKES

You Will Need

standard cupcake pan

buttercream icing, white

tip #1M

edible frosting sheet 2" (5.1 m) circles

2" (5.1 cm) round cookie cutter

rolled fondant, white

food color markers

piping gel

Techniques

Baking cupcakes, page 6

Icing Cupcakes, page 14

Buttercream and Rolled Fondant Basics, page 10

Important

Prepare the circles for the top of the cupcakes at least a day ahead of time to allow the circles to firm and not distort when placed on the iced cupcakes.

1. At least one day ahead of time, draw and color monsters on the edible frosting sheet circles using food color markers.

2. Dust the work surface with powdered sugar. Roll kneaded and softened white rolled fondant thin. Remove the edible frosting sheet circles from the paper baking. Brush the rolled fondant with piping gel. Peel back the drawn and colored circles from the paper backing. If the edible circles are sticking, slide the edible frosting sheet over the edge of a countertop to release the circles.

3. Place the edible circles on the rolled fondant. Cut the circles using a round cookie cutter the same size or slightly larger than the edible circles. Place the cut circles on parchment paper and allow to set for several hours or overnight.

4. After the circles have hardened, pipe buttercream icing on the cupcakes using a pastry bag fitted with tip #1M. Place the rolled fondant circles on the cupcakes.

★
MONSTER COOKIES

You Will Need

edible frosting sheet 3" (7.6 cm) circles

3" (7.6 cm) round cookie cutter

buttercream icing, white

tip #2A

food color markers

Techniques

Rolling and Baking Cookies, page 22

Buttercream Basics, page 10

1. Bake and cool round cookies that are the same size or slightly larger than the frosting sheets. With a black food color marker, draw monsters on the edible frosting sheet circles. Use food color markers and color in the details. Peel back the drawn and colored circle from the paper backing. If the edible sheets are sticking, slide the edible frosting sheet over the edge of a countertop to release the circles.

2. Fit a pastry bag with tip #2A. Fill the pastry bag with white buttercream icing. Pipe icing onto the cookie. Place the edible sheet on the iced cookie.

More to Know

Edible frosting sheets come both in full-size sheets that can be cut to fit nearly any project and in individually precut circles, which is what is used in this project. Edible frosting sheets are thin and very delicate. Take care to use a gentle touch when applying the edible sheet. If the sheet tears, gently press the design back together if possible. Keep the sheets covered until ready to use.

Younger Kids

Children of all ages can create patterns or pictures using food color markers on blank edible frosting sheets. Then the kids can place the colored circles on top of the rolled fondant for the cupcakes or on top of the iced cookies.

TROPICAL LUAU

★

SAND BUCKET CUPCAKES

You Will Need

jumbo cupcake pan

3" (7.6 cm) plastic sand buckets

buttercream icing, ivory

1 cup (200 g) sanding sugar

1 cup (230 g) brown sugar

tip #1A

crab sucker mold

chocolate coating, pink

sucker sticks

shell candy mold

⅛ pound (56.7 g) milk chocolate coating

½ pound (226.8 g) white chocolate coating

small brush

squeeze bottle

pearl dusting powder

soft brush for dusting

Techniques

Baking Cupcakes, page 6

Icing Cupcakes, page 14

Buttercream Basics, page 10

Coordinating Party Treats, page 26

1. Make the crab suckers following instructions for molding suckers on page 27. Melt milk chocolate coating. Brush a very thin layer of milk chocolate coating in the shell candy mold. The brush strokes should be visible, and light should be showing through when the mold is held up to a light. Allow to set at room temperature.

2. Melt white chocolate and pour it into a squeeze bottle. Fill the shell candy mold. Place the filled mold in the freezer to set. Check the mold after 5 minutes. The shells should fall from the mold. If not, return to the freezer for a few more minutes.

3. Remove the shells from the freezer and place on a sheet of parchment. Allow the shells to warm to room temperature. Using a brush with soft bristles, brush the shells with pearl dust.

More to Know

Jumbo cupcakes are baked to fit into a mini-size sand bucket. Look for these sand buckets at party supply stores or online.

SAND BUCKET CUPCAKES *(continued)*

4. Bake and cool jumbo cupcakes. Peel off the baking cup paper. Drop the baked cupcake in the plastic bucket. Gently press the cupcake so that it fills the bottom half of the bucket.

5. In a mixing bowl, combine the brown sugar and sanding sugar. Fit a pastry bag with tip #1A. Fill the bag with ivory buttercream. Pipe icing onto the top of the cupcake. Sprinkle the top with the brown sugar/sanding sugar mixture.

6. Insert the crab sucker and add the shells.

Younger Kids

Younger kids can brush piping gel on the cookie and place the rolled fondant piece on top. The hearts, flowers, and stars placed on the cookies are easy for little kids to cut and plunge. Younger children have plenty to do when assisting with these cupcakes. They can sprinkle the brown sugar/sanding sugar mixture onto the iced cupcakes and then place on the crab and arrange the seashells.

SUNGLASSES AND FLIP-FLOP COOKIES

You Will Need

flip-flop cookie cutter

sunglasses cookie cutter

piping gel

powdered sugar

rolled fondant in hot pink, purple, yellow, orange, green, blue, and black

plunger cutters, such as small heart, star, or flower

6 mm strip cutter

Techniques

Rolling and Baking Cookies, page 22

Icing cookies, page 24

Rolled Fondant Basics, page 10

1. Bake cookies following instructions on page 22. For the flip-flops, if only one cookie cutter is used (and not a pair), flip over half of the flip-flops before baking to obtain a right and left flip-flop. Allow the cookies to cool completely. Using a pastry brush, brush a very thin layer of piping gel on the cookies. Dust the work surface with powdered sugar. Roll kneaded and softened rolled fondant thin. Cut the fondant with the same cutter used in baking. Place the cut fondant on the piping gel-coated cookie. Flip over the fondant and cut the other flip-flop. Flip the fondant piece back over and place the cut fondant on the other piping gel-coated cookie.

2. To decorate the flip-flops, prepare fondant as above. Firmly press one of the plunger cutters into the rolled fondant, holding the base of the cutter. Lift the cutter and gently run your finger along the edge of the cutter to ensure the cut is clean. Push the trigger to release the cut shape. Add dots of piping gel on the flip-flops. Place the cut shapes on the flip-flops and gently press.

3. For the straps, roll kneaded and softened rolled fondant thin. Cut the fondant using a strip cutter. Attach the strips with piping gel.

4. For the sunglasses cookies, apply black rolled fondant as in step 1. Brush a small amount of piping gel around the edges of the fondant on the cookie. Prepare and cut a bright color of rolled fondant. Using a paring knife, cut out the lens of the glasses. Place on the black fondant-covered cookie. Add accents using plunger cutters following step 2 above.

FESTIVE PARTY CAKE AND TREATS

★ ★ ★

PRESENT CAKE

You Will Need

8" (20.3 cm) square cake pan

mini pizza cutter

1" (2.5 cm) round cutter

piping gel

rolled fondant in red, pink, green, lime green, light blue, and white

buttercream icing

powdered sugar

Techniques

Baking Cakes, page 4

Covering cakes with rolled fondant, page 15

Rolled Fondant Basics, page 10

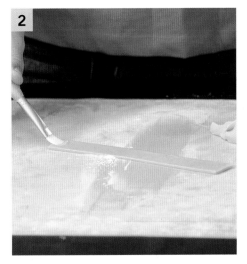

1. At least one day ahead of time, make the loops for the top of the cake. Dust the work surface with powdered sugar. Roll kneaded and softened rolled fondant thin. Using a mini pizza cutter, cut a 1" × 6" (2.5 × 15.2 cm) strip of rolled fondant.

2. Brush the end of the cut strip with piping gel.

Important

You must make the bow loops for the top of the cake and the curly streamers for the cupcakes at least a day ahead so they can harden. You can also make the dots at this time if you choose, although this is not necessary.

More to Know

This cake also looks great when iced with buttercream instead of covered with rolled fondant.

PRESENT CAKE *(continued)*

3. Fold the strip in half, being careful that the loop remains. Pinch the flat ends together and stand the loop on its side. For a full bow, make about 25 loops. Allow the loops to harden overnight before assembling the bow on the cake. If the bow loops are collapsing while being placed on their side, the fondant is not stiff enough. Tylose, a product available at cake decorating supply stores, can be added to the rolled fondant to stiffen it. Add approximately 1 tablespoon to 1 pound of rolled fondant.

4. Bake a two-layer 8" (20.3 cm) square cake, following instructions for baking on page 4. Cover the cake with white rolled fondant, following instructions on page 15. Place the cake on a cake board or a cake stand. Cut a 1" × 7" (2.5 × 17.8 cm) strip of rolled fondant for the ribbons on the side of the cake. Brush piping gel on the cake where the strip will be placed.

5. Attach the ribbon to the cake. Add a strip of rolled fondant on each side of the cake.

6. Cut various colors of rolled fondant using a small round cutter.

7. Attach the circles to the cake by placing a dot of piping gel on the cake where the circle will be placed. Add the circles and gently press in place.

8. Color buttercream icing the same color as the rolled fondant bow loops. Fill a pastry bag with the green icing. Pipe a mound of icing in the center of the cake.

9. Gently insert the pinched end of the loop into the icing. Arrange the loops in a circle around the icing mound.

10. Add layers of loops until the bow is full.

Younger Kids

Younger children can cut the circles for the polka dots and place them on the cake. They can also help arrange the bow loops on top of the cake. Let the little ones sprinkle the jimmies and add the streamers on the cupcakes.

STREAMER CUPCAKES

You Will Need

powdered sugar

standard cupcake pan

mini pizza cutter

dowel rod

rolled fondant in red, pink, green, lime green, and light blue

buttercream icing, white

jimmies in red, pink, green, lime green, and blue

tip #1M

Techniques

Baking cupcakes, page 6

Icing cupcakes, page 14

Buttercream and Rolled Fondant Basics, page 10

1. At least one day ahead of time, make the curly streamers for the cupcakes. Dust the work surface with powdered sugar. Roll kneaded and softened rolled fondant thin. Using a mini pizza cutter, cut a ¼" × 8" (6 mm × 20.3 cm) strip of rolled fondant. Wrap the cut strips around a dowel rod. Allow the streamers to harden overnight. When the streamers are hardened, gently remove from the dowel rod. The streamers can be broken into two or three pieces to create a variety of lengths.

2. Bake and cool the cupcakes. Fit a pastry bag with tip #1M. Fill the pastry bag with buttercream icing. Pipe the icing onto the cupcake.

3. Immediately add the jimmies and rolled fondant streamers.

ABOUT THE AUTHOR

AUTUMN CARPENTER'S passion for decorating started at a very young age. As a child, she would spend time at the home of her grandmother, Hall of Fame sugar artist Mildred Brand. Later, her mother, Vi Whittington, became the owner of a retail cake and candy supply shop. Her grandmother provided many recipes, while her mother instilled a work ethic, a passion for the art, and served as the best teacher and mentor that Autumn has ever had.

Autumn Carpenter has demonstrated throughout the country and served as a judge in cake decorating competitions. She has been a member, teacher, and demonstrator at the International Cake Exploration Society (ICES) for 20 years.

Autumn is co-owner of Country Kitchen SweetArt, a retail cake and candy supply store that has been owned and operated within Autumn's family for over 45 years. The business caters to walk-in store sales, catalog sales, and an online store, www.shopcountrykitchen.com.

Autumn's own line of useful tools and equipment for cake and cookie decorating can be found online as well as in many cake and candy supply stores throughout the United States and in several other countries. She has written several books, including *The Complete Photo Guide to Cake Decorating* and *The Complete Photo Guide to Cookie Decorating*.

Resources
Country Kitchen SweetArt
A one-stop shop carrying the cake and candy supplies throughout the book.

Autumn Carpenter Designs
Mini cookie cutters, perfection strips, texture mats, soccer ball texture set

Blog
www.autumncarpenter.wordpress.com

Websites
www.autumncarpenter.com
www.cookiedecorating.com
www.shopcountrykitchen.com